Out of the Treasure Chest

By V. Gilbert Beers

Illustrated by Helen Endres

MOODY PRESS • CHICAGO

What You Will Find in This Book

Library of Congress Cataloging in Publication Data

Beers, V. Gilbert (Victor Gilbert), 1928-
   Out of the Treasure Chest.
   SUMMARY: Selected Bible stories accompanied by corresponding stories involving the Muffin family demonstrate the relevance of Christian teachings to contemporary life.
   1. Bible stories, English. [1. Bible stories. 2. Christian life] I. Endres, Helen. II. Title.

BS 551.2.B4387   220.9'505   81-1601
ISBN 0-8024-6099-2
                                           AACR2

Printed in the United States of America

To Parents And Teachers

Today's child moves at a faster pace than we moved as children. He or she also moves in a world with more demands, more appeals, more sophisticated temptations, and more peer pressure. Whereas we walked, our children must run.

This running does not mean that they reach goals easier or faster. Too often our children are never faced with goals. An anxious society does not set goals – it merely races on. For example, think of the various influences shaping your child's life. Does TV set out a program of moral and spiritual values for your child and help him or her strive toward them? Does public school? Where then does your child find those goals?

Without goals your child may not arrive at the point you believe he or she should reach. The Muffin Family series of books is goal oriented. These books are based upon a program of moral and spiritual values. Each story focuses on one of them. Together they form a program of Christian life development for your child.

But while the Muffins are doing a job of educating your child for Christ, they do it in a spirit of fun and fantasy. Children WANT to read about the Muffin Family and their fun adventures. They relate easily to Maxi and Mini and their friends, who are just like them.

The Muffin Family takes a look at life's most important values. In an attic with Grandmommi, Maxi and Mini learn of things far more valuable than just "things," or possessions. A chest of family heirlooms focuses on their spiritual heritage. What greater "possession" can a child have?

Other Muffin Family books in this series are: *Through Golden Windows, Under the Tagalong Tree, With Sails to the Wind, Over Buttonwood Bridge, From Castles in the Clouds,* and *With Maxi and Mini in Muffkinland.*

ABRAHAM-
A MAN WHO BELIEVED GOD

Child of Hope

Genesis 15:1 – 18:15; 21:1 – 7

Abraham and Sarah were ashamed, for they had no children. Among their people it was a great honor to be a father or mother, especially if the child was a son. The family name and traditions went through sons and grandsons. Sons also led the family and tribe and cared for the herds of sheep, goats, and camels.

God will give us a son, Abraham and Sarah must have hoped through their younger years. But even though their younger years passed without a son, they did not lose hope.

Abraham and Sarah reached the middle years of life, and the time to have a son was passing quickly. Then God appeared to Abraham twice, each time promising a son. He even told Abraham, "You will have as many grandsons and great-grandsons as there are stars in the sky, and they will come through the son I will give you."

Abraham and Sarah believed God. They would not lose hope that God would give them a son, even though they were getting older.

"But how?" they wondered. Then Sarah had an idea. Among their people a woman who had no children could tell her servant girl to live with her husband as a wife. If the servant girl had a child, the woman could claim that child as her own.

Sarah told her servant girl, Hagar, to live with Abraham as a wife. In time she and Abraham had a son, just as they all hoped she would. Now Sarah and Abraham believed that this son, whom they named Ishmael, was the son for whom they had hoped.

"No, he is not," God told Abraham one day. "I have promised a son to you and Sarah."

But how can we still hope for our own son? Abraham thought. *I am ninety-nine years old, and Sarah is ninety. We are too old now to have our own son.*

"You WILL have a son!" God promised. "You will name him Isaac."

Later, when Abraham and Sarah were sure they were too old to have a child, God gave them the son He had promised. They named him Isaac, as God had said that they should. What they had hoped for in the early, middle, and later years of their lives had now come to pass in their old age. The son that God had promised was theirs at last.

WHAT DO YOU THINK?
What this story teaches: Never lose hope that God will keep His promises.

1. Was it easy for Abraham and Sarah to keep their hope alive when they were young and could have children? Did it grow easier or harder for them to hope for a child as they grew older?
2. When God promises something, should we EVER doubt that it will happen? Look for His promises as you read His Word, the Bible. Accept them as your own and never lose hope that He will keep them.

The Tree of Hope

"What you need is some fruit from the Tree of Hope," said the king's royal physician, Dr. BoBo.

King Maxi tried to smile, but he was so sad. "I certainly need something," he said softly. "I have lost hope that Princess Mini will ever come home as she promised when she left."

"Eat the fruit from this tree, and you will have hope once more," said the royal physician.

"Oh, all right," said the king. "Order my royal attendants to saddle my horse, and I will eat of this fruit."

Before long King Maxi rode from the castle, through the royal gardens and forests, until at last he came to the Tree of Hope. But there was no fruit on the tree, only bright red and yellow leaves, for it was autumn.

"There will never be fruit on this tree," the king complained. "And Princess Mini will never come home." Then he returned sadly to the castle.

Each day the king watched from the castle window for Princess Mini. He saw the bright leaves of autumn turn brown and flutter to the ground. Then he saw

8

them blow away with the winter winds that swept through the forest.

The first snows of winter brought new sadness to the king. He felt even more hopeless, sure that the princess would never return.

"Search again for fruit on the Tree of Hope," his royal physician advised. "It will give you new hope."

Again King Maxi rode from the castle, through the royal gardens and forests, until at last he came to the Tree of Hope. But there was no fruit on it, only the soft white snow that lay upon its branches, for it was winter.

"There will never be fruit on this tree," the king complained. "And Princess Mini will never come home." Then he returned to the castle.

Each day the king watched from the castle window for Princess Mini. He saw the winter snow drift along the fences and trees, then melt with the first warm sunshine of early spring. Before long, green shoots came up through the dead leaves of last autumn, and birds began to sing in the forest. Wildflowers bloomed again, and the soft breezes of spring sighed to the king. But the princess had still not returned. The king felt even more hopeless, sure that she would never come home.

"Search again for fruit on the Tree of Hope," said the royal physician. "It will give you new hope."

Again King Maxi rode from the castle, through the royal gardens and forests, until at last he came to the Tree of Hope. But there was no fruit on it, only tender green leaves and among them soft, sweet-smelling pink blossoms, for it was spring.

"There will never be fruit on this tree," said the king. "And Princess Mini will never come home." Then he returned sadly to the castle.

Each day the king watched from the castle window for Princess Mini. He saw the pink blossoms fall to the ground and the tender green leaves grow into the large beautiful leaves of summer. The grass grew tall in the meadows, and the summer sun smiled down. At last, summer was in its full glory. But the king felt even more hopeless, sure that the princess would never return.

"Search again for fruit on the Tree of Hope," said the royal physician. "It will give you new hope."

Again King Maxi rode from the castle, through the royal gardens and forests, until at last he came to the Tree of Hope. This time the king smiled as he looked up into the tree, for there was bright red fruit hanging on its branches.

"Perhaps the princess will return," the king said as he stood quietly looking at the fruit.

"Why don't you pick some for me?" a voice called to King Maxi. He turned quickly and saw Princess Mini, riding toward him on the path.

"Princess Mini!" the king shouted. "You have come back!"

"Of course," the princess said calmly. "I promised that I would, didn't I? Surely you didn't lose hope that I would keep my promise, did you?"

King Maxi smiled a weak little smile. "Well, perhaps just a little," he said. "Now why don't we eat our fruit as we ride together to the castle?"

"I HOPEed you would say that!" said the princess.

LET'S TALK ABOUT THIS

What this story teaches: We must always keep hope high that good promises will come true.

1. Had Princess Mini promised to come back to the castle? Why then do you think King Maxi lost hope that she would return?

2. Do you ever lose hope that a promise will come true? If it is a good promise, is it right to lose hope? How is the Bible like the Tree of Hope? Will God keep every promise He has made to us through His Word?

11

Family Divided

Genesis 16:1-16; 21:8-21

"Get rid of her!" Sarah screamed at her husband, Abraham. "And get rid of that son of hers!"

Abraham was upset to hear Sarah say such things. "That son" was also his son Ishmael. Sarah had even claimed him as her son.

Abraham and Sarah had not been able to have a son. As the years passed, they kept hoping that God's promise of a son would come true. But how?

Then Sarah told her servant girl, Hagar, to live with Abraham as a wife. The child she would have would become Sarah's child.

But when Hagar knew that she was going to have a child, she grew proud and looked down on Sarah. Then Sarah beat her, and Hagar ran away.

The Lord spoke to Hagar and told her to return to Sarah and be obedient to her. Hagar did, but she still taunted Sarah. The two made life miserable for each other and for Abraham. It was a family divided.

Things grew worse when Sarah had her own son, Isaac. No longer was she interested in Hagar's son, Ishmael. Abraham also grew much more interested in Isaac. Hagar soon realized that this new baby would take the place of her son, Ishmael. Isaac, not Ishmael, would become Abraham's heir and would lead the family when Abraham was gone. Isaac, not Ishmael, would receive Abraham's love and attention from now on.

This made Hagar and Ishmael angry and hurt and jealous. At a special party that Abraham gave for Isaac, Ishmael began to make fun of him.

Sarah was furious when she saw this. "Get rid of Hagar," she screamed at her husband, Abraham. "And get rid of that son of hers!"

Abraham was trapped, caught between his real wife and her son and Hagar and her son. His family was divided, and he must choose between some of them. Only God's wisdom could help him make the right choice.

WHAT DO YOU THINK?

What this story teaches: When someone is forced to choose between one family member or another, God's wisdom alone can help him or her make the right choice.

1. What caused Sarah to turn against Hagar and Ishmael? What usually causes jealousy between family members?
2. If you had to choose between one family member or another, where would you go for help?

Play Ball

"You heard me!" BoBo shouted at Maxi. "If you don't let me pitch, I'll take my ball and go home!"

"And you heard me, too!" Pookie shouted as loud as BoBo had done. "If you don't let me pitch, I'll take my catcher's mitt and go home!"

Maxi gulped. He looked at BoBo and then at Pookie. Both were good pitchers and both were good friends.

"That's not fair!" Maxi complained. "You're asking me to choose between two good friends."

"We can play without one of them," Charlie advised.

"You can't play without a ball," BoBo answered snootily.

"And you can't play without a catcher's mitt," Pookie added, just as snootily.

14

"Looks like you two spoiled kids are saying we can't play ball," Charlie added. "With this kind of team spirit, we'll wind up at the bottom of the city dump leagues."

"You're the captain, Maxi," said BoBo. "All you have to do is choose me as pitcher, and we can get started."

"Without a catcher's mitt?" asked Pookie. "So you had better choose me, Captain Maxi!"

Maxi sat down on the pitcher's mound, his chin in his hands. What could he do? How could he choose between his two good friends? And how could they play ball without a ball or a catcher's mitt?

"I'd send them both to the showers," Charlie advised.

"That would send the rest of us with them," said Tony, who had been listening to the whole thing. "The truth is we need BOTH the ball and catcher's mitt. Right?"

"Right!" said Maxi. "And we really need BOTH BoBo and Pookie. But I can't choose one, or the other will leave. So now what do we do?"

BoBo and Pookie stood like rubber statues, waiting for Maxi to choose one of them. All the other team- mates looked angry as they watched BoBo and Pookie.

"OK, I have an idea," said Charlie. "Let's talk some sense into these two turkeys. If either of you is chosen the other one will go home. Right?"

"Right!" said BoBo and Pookie together.

"So, if BoBo is chosen, he can pitch to a catcher without a mitt. Right?" said Charlie.

"Well, ah...uh..." BoBo tried to answer. But he realized that he couldn't, for no one would catch without a mitt.

"And, if Pookie is chosen, he can throw bubble gum or candy wrappers into the catcher's mitt. Right?" Charlie needled.

"Well, ah...uh..." Pookie tried to answer. But he realized that he couldn't, for no one would play ball without a ball.

"So, you see, my spoiled little children, this ball game is all over, thanks to your selfishness." Charlie needled them even more. "You're putting one of your best friends on the spot, right in the middle between you, and he can't choose one of you above the other."

"So what's your brilliant idea, Charlie?" asked Maxi.

"Not brilliant, just plain old horse sense," said Charlie. "We flip this penny. Heads, Pookie pitches. Tails, BoBo pitches. Right, guys?"

"OK by me," said Pookie.

"Me, too," said BoBo.

Charlie gave the penny a high flip into the air and let it land on the ground near the pitcher's mound. But it landed on edge and began to roll. Everybody ran after the penny to see how it would land.

The penny rolled behind the pitcher's mound and fell into a small crack in the ground, staying upright.

"Oh, no!" shouted Maxi. "Even the coin won't choose!"

"Yes, it did!" said Charlie. "It's telling us exactly who to choose."

"It is?" asked Maxi. "What does it say?"

"That Pookie should pitch half of the game and BoBo the other half!"

It was so simple that no one had thought of it. "Great idea!" said Pookie.

"Play ball!" said BoBo.

So they did.

LET'S TALK ABOUT THIS
What this story teaches: Sometimes we are forced to choose between friends or family members. The best choice may be not to choose one above the other.

1. Why was it so hard for Maxi to choose between two friends? Have you ever found it hard to choose between two friends or family members? What did you do?

2. What did the coin in this story teach about choosing one friend or family member above another? How does this remind you of the sad choice Abraham had to make? How do you think God would have you choose today?

Obeying Without Question

Genesis 22:1-19

As the years passed, Isaac grew taller and stronger. Abraham and Sarah loved their only son dearly, more than anything else in the world.

One day God tested Abraham to see if he loved his son too much. Would he give up his beloved son if God told him to? Would he obey God completely?

"Abraham! Take your only son, whom you love so much, to the land of Moriah," God said. "Offer him on an altar as a burnt offering."

Abraham was stunned at God's orders. Isaac? His beloved Isaac, for whom he had waited a lifetime? Why would God want to have him burn his only beloved son upon an altar? Why?

Abraham must have asked why a hundred times early the next morning as he split the wood for the

18

fire. But he saddled his donkey and left for Moriah with Isaac and two young servant boys. It was a long way from Beer-sheba to Moriah, so they did not arrive until the third day.

Abraham must have kept asking why as he traveled to Moriah. But not once did he think of disobeying God. Not once did he refuse to trust God to do what was best.

"Stay here with the donkey," Abraham told the servant boys. "Isaac and I will go into the mountain to make an offering to God. Then we'll be back."

Isaac was young and strong, so he carried the wood for the fire. Abraham carried the long, sharp knife and the flint, which he would use to start the fire. Together they climbed Mount Moriah.

By this time Isaac was wondering about this offering they were to make. "We have the wood and flint to make a fire," he told Abraham. "But where is the lamb for the burnt offering?"

"God will take care of that," Abraham answered softly.

At last the two arrived at the top of Mount Moriah and found the place where God had told Abraham to go. Abraham gathered stones and made an altar with them. Then he laid the wood upon the altar.

With a heavy heart, Abraham tied Isaac's hands and feet, telling him about God's commands as he did. Isaac listened carefully. He also must have wondered why, but he willingly let his father lay him on the altar.

Slowly Abraham lifted the knife to plunge it into his beloved son. He would do anything God told him to do, even give up the son he loved so much. But at that moment a voice called from heaven.

"Abraham! Abraham!"

"Yes, Lord!" Abraham answered anxiously.

"Put that knife down. You must not hurt young Isaac," the Lord said. "Now I know that you will obey Me completely, for you would even give up your beloved son for Me."

While the Lord spoke, Abraham saw a ram caught by its horns in a nearby bush. When the Lord had finished speaking, Abraham took the ram and sacrificed it upon the altar he had built for his son.

Once again the Lord spoke to Abraham. "You have obeyed Me without question," the Lord told him. "Because you have, I will do wonderful things through the thousands of grandsons and great-grandsons that you will have through Isaac."

Abraham quietly thanked God for His goodness. Then he and Isaac went down the mountain to the two servant boys waiting for them.

"Anything unusual happen up there?" the boys may have asked, as curious boys do.

Abraham would have smiled at Isaac, who gave a big smile for his father. "Perhaps," Abraham answered.

Then the four headed back to Beer-sheba.

WHAT DO YOU THINK?
What this story teaches: Obey God without question, exactly as He tells you to do.

1. What did God ask Abraham to do? Did Abraham argue with God about it? Did he even ask God why, or did he merely wonder why?
2. Why should we obey God exactly as He wants? Why not obey only part of God's orders? Which half would you obey, the half you want to do or the half you don't want to do?

Shopping

"It's so much fun shopping with you, Mommi," said Mini Muffin.

"It's fun to have you with me, Mini," Mommi answered. "I do hope you won't be bored today, though. I must find a new dress, shoes, and purse, so it may take a while for those things."

Mini was absolutely and positively sure that she would not be bored. She would pretend that each new dress Mommi tried on was something special that she would wear to a birthday party that a prince was giving in his castle.

"This one would look neat as I step from the coach and curtsy to the prince." Mini giggled as she watched Mommi check out the first dress before some mirrors.

"And this would look great as I dine with the prince at the royal birthday party," she whispered about the second one.

For the third dress Mini dreamed of walking in the castle garden with the prince, for the fourth she dreamed that she and the prince were visiting His Majesty the king and Her Majesty the queen in the royal throne room, and for the fifth she dreamed that she and the prince were sitting by a fountain, splashing their bare feet in the water.

But when Mommi came from the dressing room with number six, Mini gave a big yawn and slumped down into her chair. She couldn't think of another thing to do with the prince, and she was really tired of him anyway. Right now she would settle for just plain Maxi or Pookie or Maria.

Mommi noticed Mini wiggling and slumping in her chair. She also noticed Mini's big yawn.

"I was afraid of that," Mommi whispered. Then she had an idea. Perhaps Mini would enjoy the toy department while Mommi finished her shopping.

"Do you mind?" Mommi asked Mrs. Tinker in the toy department.

"Mini can come here anytime," said Mrs. Tinker.

Before Mommi left, she told Mini exactly what to do. "I'll go back to the dress department, then on to get my shoes, and then my purse," said Mommi. "But I want you to wait right here in the toy department until I come for you. Do you understand?"

"Yes, Mommi," said Mini. "I will be here."

Mini started in the dollhouse section, then went to look at games, and then to the miniatures, and then to see the stuffed animals. But after she had seen all the toys once, it wasn't as much fun to look at them again. It was even less fun the third time and just plain boring the fourth time.

"I can't wait here all day for Mommi," Mini said to herself, "even though she told me to. I'll slip over to the dress department and watch her again."

But Mommi wasn't in the dress department when Mini came there. Mini went to the shoe department, but Mommi had already bought the shoes and had gone on. By the time Mini reached the purses, Mommi had bought hers and had gone back to the toy department for Mini. And by the time Mini had reached the toy department, Mommi had gone back to the dress department to look for Mini.

By the time Mommi and Mini had chased each other around the departments three times, Mommi was losing patience. "Please tell Mini to wait here in the toy department if she gets back before I do," Mommi told Mrs. Tinker. "Please tell her that wait means EXACTLY that."

Mrs. Tinker smiled. "I will tell her," she said.

Much later, when Mommi had gone around the departments once more, she found a tired little Mini, waiting EXACTLY at the place she had said.

"I'm sorry, Mommi," said Mini. "I...I thought we would save time if I went to find you."

"Oh, Mini, I had so wanted us to have time for ice cream at the Candy Counter, but now I must go home to get dinner started," said Mommi.

"If only I had done EXACTLY as you told me to do we would have had time," Mini said. "But I certainly will next time."

Mommi smiled. "Yes, I really think you will," she said. Then she and Mini went home.

LET'S TALK ABOUT THIS
What this story teaches: True obedience is to obey exactly.

1. Did Abraham obey God exactly? Did Mini? Why not?
2. Why is it so important to obey God and parents exactly? Why not obey only what we want to obey and do the rest the way we want?

DAVID-A KING, GOOD AND BAD

A King Who Wanted to Help

2 Samuel 9

One day King David began to think about his best friend, Jonathan, who had been killed in battle. He remembered how he and Jonathan had loved each other, as best friends do. He remembered also how he had promised Jonathan that he would be kind to Jonathan's family when he became king.

But who are they, and where are they? King David wondered. *Are any of Jonathan's children alive? I must find out.*

King David asked the right people and found that there was a man named Ziba who would know. Ziba had been an important servant of Jonathan's father, King Saul. So the king called for Ziba to come to the palace.

"I want to show kindness to Jonathan's children, if any are still alive," the king explained. "I promised before God that I would."

"Only one son is still living," Ziba told King David. "He is crippled. His name is Mephibosheth."

"Where may I find him?" David asked.

"At Machir's home in Lo-debar," Ziba answered.

The king immediately sent some men there to bring Mephibosheth back to him. Mephibosheth was much afraid as he bowed before the king, for he thought that he would be killed. He was not only the son of Jonathan, David's best friend, but the grandson of King Saul, David's worst enemy. Kings at that time often tried to kill the sons and grandsons of kings who had ruled before them so they could not try to take their thrones from them.

"You must not be afraid of me," King David explained. "I do not want to hurt you. I want to help you, as I promised your father, Jonathan, I would. I am giving you all the land that belonged to your grandfather, Saul."

Mephibosheth could hardly believe his ears. "But I am a nobody!" he told King David.

That did not matter to the king. He expected nothing in return. He did not care that Mephibosheth was poor and crippled and had nothing to give him.

"You will also live here at the palace and eat at my

royal table," King David told Mephibosheth.

Then the king called for Ziba. "I have given Mephibosheth all the land that once belonged to King Saul," he said. "You and your sons and servants will farm this land for him, but he will live here at the palace with me."

Ziba bowed low before King David. He had fifteen sons and twenty servants. "We will all do as you have commanded," he promised.

So, from that time on, Mephibosheth and his young son, Mica, lived at the palace of King David. He ate food at the royal table. And Ziba, with his fifteen sons and twenty servants, farmed the land that King David had given to Mephibosheth.

The king treated Mephibosheth like one of his own sons. A nobody had become a royal prince again. And King David was very happy that he could show kindness to someone who could not repay him.

WHAT DO YOU THINK?
What this story teaches: It is good to show kindness to others, especially to those who cannot repay us.

1. Why was Mephibosheth afraid to come before King David? What did David do for him?
2. Could Mephibosheth repay the king for his kindness? Did this keep the king from being kind to him? Why not?
3. Why should it bring special happiness to show kindness to those who cannot repay us?

A Special Day

"This is the most be-yoo-tiful day we've had for a long time," Mini crooned. "May we do something special today?"

Poppi put down his cup and finished the last bite of egg on his plate. "A be-yoo-tiful Saturday and four eager, anxious Muffins. Now what could we do to make this a special day?"

"The beach!" Maxi suggested, almost shouting.

"A day at Fun Village Amusement Park!" Mini shouted, just as loud as Maxi.

"A peaceful drive in the country," said Mommi. "Or a picnic in the park."

Poppi chuckled. "Three people and four ideas," he said. "Should I add a fifth?"

"Is it more special than ours?" asked Mini.

"Would we have more fun doing it?" asked Maxi.

"Yes and no," Poppi answered.

"How can it be yes and no both?" Maxi wondered.

"Yes, it is more special than our other ideas," Poppi answered. "Yes, you will have more fun than at an amusement park or the beach or a picnic. No, you will not think it is special or more fun when I mention it."

"Now we ARE curious," said Maxi.

"Yes, Poppi, tell us what it is," Mini added.

"I'll give you some clues," said Poppi. "First, it will be doing something special for others."

Maxi and Mini thought for a moment or two. But they needed more clues than that.

"Second, it is doing something together as a Muffin Family," said Poppi.

But still Maxi and Mini could not think what it might be. "You'll have to give us another clue," said Maxi.

"OK, here's a third clue," said Poppi. "We'll be doing something for people who can't do special things for us in return. And how about a fourth clue while we're at it? These are people who can't go to the beach, or to an amusement park, or on a picnic."

"What kind of people can't do those things?" asked Mini.

"I know," said Maxi. "The people in the nursing home. We're going to sing for them again or do something else for them."

"Maxi guessed it," said Poppi. "But this isn't my decision. It's our decision. What do you say?"

Mini and Maxi looked sad.

"Well, it really doesn't sound like much fun," said Maxi.

"And I did want to go to the Fun Village," said Mini. "But I think we should sing for the people at the nursing home."

"And why don't we read some Bible verses to them?" added Maxi.

"A third idea," said Mommi. "I'll call to see if any-one has a birthday today. If so, we'll take a birthday cake and sing 'Happy Birthday.' "

On the way home that afternoon Maxi and Mini were chattering like squirrels.

"Did you see the tears on Mrs. Crowley's face when we sang 'Happy Birthday' to her?" Mini bubbled. "And how happy everyone looked when we read Bible verses and sang to them?"

"Yeah, and did you notice Mr. Mack's face when he asked if Mini and I really wanted to come today or if Mommi and Poppi made us come?"

"Did you want to go?" asked Poppi.

"Well, yes and no," Maxi answered, with a laugh. "No, I didn't want to give up the fun things we talked about. Yes, I wanted to make others happy, especially since they couldn't do a thing to make us happy."

"This was a special day," said Mini. "I'm glad we went. We can go to the beach some other day."

"And we will," Poppi added.

LET'S TALK ABOUT THIS

What this story teaches: It is fun to do things for others, but it is especially fun to do things for those who can't "repay" us.

1. Why do you think Mini and Maxi had fun at the nursing home? Why was it even more fun to help people who couldn't help them?

2. Can you think of some people who can't help you when you help them? Can you think of some ways to make them happy? Will you do it? How is this like the things God does for us? Can we ever repay Him for all He does?

The King's Sin

2 Samuel 11:1 – 12:14

Of all the kings of Israel, King David was the best. He loved the Lord and tried to please Him. He wrote many of the beautiful psalms in the Bible.

But sometimes the best people do things that are terribly wrong, often hurting those around them. Even King David did that.

It was springtime in Jerusalem. David's army had gone to war. Uriah was one of the young officers who went with the army, leaving his beautiful wife, Bath-sheba, behind in Jerusalem.

David saw Bath-sheba one evening and was sure that she was the most beautiful woman in the world. The more he thought about Bath-sheba, the more he wanted her, even though she was married to a loyal army officer.

At last he could stand it no longer. He sent for her and pretended that she was his wife, not Uriah's. Thus the great King David sinned.

Sin always makes things worse, not better. Bath-sheba let David know one day that they would have a baby. The king realized now what a mess he had made. But instead of saying, "I'm sorry, I have sinned," he brought Uriah home from the war and tried to get him to stay with his wife. He wanted Uriah to think this was his child.

But Uriah was such a loyal army officer that he would not go to the comforts of his home while his friends were fighting in a war. David's plan failed.

Desperate now, the king went from a great sin to an even greater one. He ordered Uriah's commanding officer to send him into a place in battle where he would be killed.

When the news came back to Jerusalem that Uriah was dead, the king was free to marry Bath-sheba. But David learned that sin leaves ugly scars. When a person hurts others around him to get what he wants, he himself may later be hurt by what he did.

One day a prophet of God named Nathan came to see the king. He told the king a story about a rich man who had a feast. Instead of using his own lamb for the feast, the rich man forced a poor man to give up his pet lamb and killed it for the feast.

David was furious. "That man will be punished!" he vowed. Then Nathan sadly told the king that he was that rich man. He had murdered an innocent man to steal his one pet lamb–his beautiful wife.

King David saw it all now. He had sinned, not once, but twice. He had even murdered to get what he wanted.

"I have sinned!" he cried out. "I have sinned against the Lord!"

It was true. David's sin had hurt Uriah. It had hurt Bath-sheba. It had hurt him. It had hurt the baby that he and Bath-sheba would have, for Nathan said it would die. But most of all, David's sin hurt the Lord, as all sin does.

David's story ended better than some stories do, for he begged the Lord to forgive him. The scars of his sin stayed with him, but the Lord forgave. Later, David and Bath-sheba would have a baby who would be the next king of Israel.

WHAT DO YOU THINK?
What this story teaches: When we sin by taking what we want, we hurt the other person, ourselves, and the Lord.

1. How did King David hurt Uriah? How did he hurt Bath-sheba? How did he hurt himself? How did he hurt the Lord?
2. When Nathan told the king about his sin, what did the king do? What is the best thing to do when we realize we have sinned against someone?

The Royal Feast

"Saddle our horses, Sir Pookie," King Maxi ordered. "We are going to search for a lamb for the royal feast."

"With horses?" asked Sir Pookie. "Do you expect to find it among someone else's flocks?"

"Perhaps," said King Maxi. "Who knows where we may find it?"

Sir Pookie was afraid to ask more questions. Knights were important, but not as important as kings. Sometimes knights who asked too many questions were put into jail or forced to work hard for the king. Sir Pookie didn't like jail, and he certainly didn't like to work hard, so he stopped asking questions.

Before long Sir Pookie and King Maxi rode across the drawbridge of the castle into the country. They passed by the rich house of Sir Anthony of Squireshire, whom the king called simply Tony; the estate of Sir Charles of Willow Manor, whom the king called Charlie; and the great house of Sir William of Worcestershire Manor, whom the king called Big Bill Bluffalo.

"Have you seen the lamb you wish?" Sir Pookie asked.

"Not yet," said King Maxi. "When I see it I will know it is the right one, for it will be the finest lamb in the land."

On and on rode King Maxi and Sir Pookie. They were far into the country now, where poor people lived in little huts. "How do you expect to find the best lamb of the land out here?" Sir Pookie asked.

"Who knows?" said the king. "It could be anywhere, even in that miserable little hut over there." King Maxi pointed to a tiny hut where a very poor family lived.

"Well, there is a lamb there, playing with that little girl," said Sir Pookie.

King Maxi stopped his horse to watch the girl play with the lamb. They ran and jumped and had fun

together. Then the girl picked up the lamb in her arms and hugged it.

"You are worth more than anything to me," the girl said with a giggle. "I love you like a dearest friend."

King Maxi turned to Sir Pookie. "That is the lamb I want for the royal feast!" he said. "We will take it back to the palace now!"

"But, Your Highness, it is a pet lamb," Sir Pookie argued, forgetting he could be put into jail or forced to work hard.

"If you won't get that lamb for me, I'll get it myself," said the king. Then he rode into the yard where the little girl was playing.

"Your Majesty," the girl said with a curtsy. "What may I do for you?"

"Give me your lamb for my royal feast," the king demanded.

The little girl clutched her pet lamb closely. Tears streamed down her cheeks.

"Oh, no! No, not my pet lamb! Please don't do such a horrible thing," the girl cried. "It is like a sister to me. You can't kill it. You can't! You can't!"

"Seize that lamb, Sir Pookie!" the king ordered.

Sir Pookie stood still, for he was sure that he could not take the poor lamb away.

"Seize it, or I'll throw you into prison!" the king shouted. So Sir Pookie seized the lamb from the little girl and rode for the castle with the king, leaving the poor girl screaming and crying as she ran down the road after them.

When they reached the castle, King Maxi called for the royal executioner to kill the lamb and prepare it for the royal feast. But before the executioner came, Princess Mini walked up.

"Guess what happened while you were gone?" she asked the king. "A wicked boy stole our poor Tuff and plans to make catburgers with her."

King Maxi was furious. "I'll boil him in oil, I'll throw him in the worst prison, I'll...I'll..." The king couldn't think of anything bad enough for that wicked fellow.

"Before you blow a royal fuse, tell me why you're so angry," Princess Mini asked.

"Because Tuff was our pet," said the king. "I love her like a sister. Now, who did this terrible thing?"

"You!!" said Princess Mini. "But it wasn't Tuff that was stolen; it was a dear little pet lamb. You stole it from that poor little girl who followed you and is standing over there. Now give it back to her before I fry you for the royal feast."

King Maxi was stunned. What had he done? What if someone had made his Tuff into catburgers? He would be heartbroken. Then King Maxi looked at the poor little girl. Tears were still streaming down her face.

King Maxi took the lamb into his arms and carried it to the little girl. "I'm terribly sorry," he said. "Please forgive me."

The girl smiled, took the lamb into her arms, and hugged it. Then the king invited her to stay for the royal feast—hamburgers, fries, and shakes.

LET'S TALK ABOUT THIS
What this story teaches: It is wrong to take what we want when that hurts someone else.

1. How does this story remind you of the story of David and Bath-sheba? How was King Maxi like King David? How was Princess Mini like the prophet Nathan?

2. Have you ever wanted something so much you were willing to hurt someone to get it? If you ever do, what will you remember? And if you do, pray that Jesus will help you do what is right!

ELIJAH-POWER AND PROBLEMS

Fire from Heaven

1 Kings 18

For three years there had been no rain in the land. Crops would not grow, so there was almost no food. People all over the land were hungry. By this time King Ahab should have realized that God had stopped the rain. He should have realized that Elijah had told the truth three years earlier when he had said that God would stop the rain. But he refused to believe those things.

The wicked Queen Jezebel also refused to believe them. She hated God's prophet and wanted to kill him. She thought that Baal and Asherah were the true gods and that their prophets were the true prophets.

Hundreds of those false prophets ate good food with the king and queen. Elijah ate simple bread with a poor widow. The false prophets tried to get the people to worship their idols. Elijah tried to get the people to worship God.

Some people worshiped the idols of the false prophets. Others worshiped God. Still others tried to worship both.

One day God spoke to Elijah. It was time to make the people choose between God and the false gods.

"Bring those prophets of Baal and Asherah to Mount Carmel," Elijah told the king. The king was not sure what would happen, but he did as Elijah said. The people of Israel also gathered to see what would happen.

"How long will you serve both idols and God?" Elijah asked the people. "If the Lord is the true God, follow Him! If Baal is the true god, follow him!"

Then Elijah told his plan. A young bull would be laid on the wood of the altar, without fire under it. The prophets of Baal would go first, calling upon their god to send fire to burn the offering. Then Elijah would do the same, calling upon his God to send fire. Whoever sent the fire was the true God.

The 450 prophets of Baal went first. They placed the young bull they had chosen upon the wood of the altar. Then they begged Baal to send fire.

All through the morning those false prophets called to Baal, begging him to send fire. But nothing happened. By noon Elijah began to make fun of them. "Shout louder!" he teased. "He may be away somewhere!"

The false prophets did shout louder. They also cut themselves with knives and swords. They kept on doing those things until evening, the time when the people of God made their offerings to Him.

"Come to me!" Elijah called to the people of Israel.

When they gathered around, Elijah rebuilt the altar that had once been used for offerings to God. Then he dug a trench around the altar and put the wood and the meat of the other young bull upon the altar.

"Now pour four barrels of water over the wood and meat," Elijah ordered. Some people did as he said.

"Do it again," Elijah ordered. Once more some people poured four barrels of water over the wood and meat.

"Once more!" Elijah ordered. By this time water ran into the trench.

Then Elijah prayed to the Lord. "Lord of Abraham, Isaac, and Jacob, prove now that You are the true God of Israel and that I am Your true prophet," he prayed. "Answer me, O Lord!"

Fire flashed from the heavens and burned up the meat, the wood, the stones, and even the water in the ditch. When the people of Israel saw that, they fell upon the ground. "The Lord is God! The Lord is God!" they shouted.

"Then kill those false prophets!" shouted Elijah. The people immediately captured the false prophets, and Elijah executed them below at the brook Kishon.

"You had better eat now," Elijah told the king, "for a great rainstorm is coming."

The king ate and drank while Elijah climbed to the top of the mountain and prayed with his face between his knees. He ordered his servant seven times to look out over the sea to watch for a cloud.

At last the servant told Elijah, "There is a little cloud about the size of a man's hand coming from the sea."

"Then tell the king to get into his chariot and head

toward home, for the rain is coming," Elijah told the servant.

The king jumped into his chariot and raced for his palace. But the Lord gave Elijah such strength that he ran faster than the king's chariot, reaching the entrance of the city before him.

WHAT DO YOU THINK?
What this story teaches: Our God is a God who listens to His people.
1. What did the false prophets ask their god, Baal, to do? Did he? What did Elijah ask God to do? Did He?
2. What does this tell you about idols and other false gods? What does it tell you about God?

Someone Who Listens

"Mini, please, I can't talk with you now. Can't you see that I'm on the phone?"

"Sorry, Mommi."

Mini often wondered why people like Mommi said they were on the phone. It looked to her like Mommi was on a chair, talking to the phone.

Mini wandered from the kitchen to the living room. There was a newspaper sitting in a chair. Mini was quite sure that Poppi was sitting behind it.

"Poppi?"

"Hmnf?"

"Poppi?"

"Snumff?"

"Poppi."

"Whmnfp?"

"Poppi."

"Mini! Can't you see that I'm reading the newspaper? Find something to do. I can't talk with you now."

Mini wandered from the living room to the backyard. She was thinking about Poppi's newspaper. It must be very interesting! She had tried to read it one time, but the part she read was about the legal problems of condominium ownership, and she had not thought it interesting at all.

Maxi was playing with Pookie and Charlie in the tree house when Mini called up to him.

"Maxi!"

"Get lost, kid!" Maxi shouted to her. "Can't you see that we have a very imPAWtant meeting?"

Mini hung her head and sat down in the shade of a big tree. A tear came into her eye as she watched Ruff playing with a neighbor dog.

"Ruff, come here!" Mini called. But Ruff was having so much fun that he paid no attention at all to Mini. When Mini tried to talk to Tuff, who was sunning on the patio, Tuff lifted one sleepy eyelid and then plopped it closed again.

"My own dog and cat won't talk to me!" Mini wailed. "Nobody will talk to me! I must be a total blob!"

Mini shuffled up to her room, plopped on her bed and cried. "Nobody!" she sniffed. "Not my poppi or mommi or my brother. Not even my dog or cat!"

After Mini had sniffed and snorted for a while, she began to straighten out the things on her dresser. She put her mirror and combs together neatly, quite unlike the way they usually were. Then she put her pack of Bible memory verses neatly by the comb. But as she did, she noticed the verse she had been memorizing: *"Call unto Me, and I will answer thee, and show thee great and mighty things, which thou knowest not"* (Jeremiah 33:3).

Mini took the little card from the memory pack and read the verse several times.

Wow! That means that God is never too busy talking on the phone, or reading the newspaper, or playing in a tree house, Mini thought. *That means He will listen right now.*

So Mini began to talk to God. And she was sure He was listening to every word she said!

LET'S TALK ABOUT THIS
What this story teaches: God will listen to us at all times, even when others will not.

1. Why did Mini feel as she did? How do you feel when everyone seems too busy to talk to you? 2. Have you ever thought that no one was interested in talking to you? What did Mini learn from her Bible memory verse? What did you learn from it? Will you remember it when you want to talk and you think nobody wants to talk with you?

A Quiet Voice

1 Kings 19: 1-18

"I'll kill you!" Queen Jezebel told Elijah. "I'll kill you by tomorrow evening!"

The wicked queen was furious when King Ahab told her how Elijah had made the prophets of Baal look foolish and ordered them killed. How dare he do that to her and her prophets?

Elijah was afraid when he heard the queen's threats. So he ran away. First he went through the desert to Beer-sheba. Leaving his servant there, he went on south to Mount Horeb, sometimes called Mount Sinai, far from the wicked queen. He hid in a lonely cave in the mountain.

"What are you doing here?" the Lord asked Elijah one day.

"I have worked hard for You, Lord," Elijah answered. "But the people have not listened to me. They have torn down Your altars and killed Your prophets. Now I'm the only one of Your prophets left, and they are trying to kill me, too."

"Go outside," God told Elijah. "Stand there and wait for Me."

Elijah stepped outside the cave, waiting for some sign from the Lord. Suddenly a powerful windstorm swept around the mountain. It tore rocks loose and sent them tumbling down its sides. But the Lord was not in the wind.

The wind died down. Elijah waited again for some sign of the Lord's presence. Suddenly the mountain began to tremble from a mighty earthquake. But the Lord was not in the earthquake.

When the earthquake had stopped, Elijah stayed waiting for some sign that the Lord was there. A great fire began. Surely the Lord would be in that! But He was not.

The fire quieted down and went out. Elijah still waited for some sign that the Lord was there, speaking to him.

Suddenly Elijah heard a soft whisper. It was the gentle voice of the Lord. Elijah stood at the entrance of the cave and listened.

"What are you doing here?" the Lord asked Elijah again.

Once more Elijah told the Lord. "I have worked hard for You, but the people have not listened to me. They have torn down Your altars and killed Your prophets. Now I'm the only one of Your prophets left, and they are trying to kill me, too."

"It's time for you to go home," the Lord told Elijah. "On the way, you will anoint Hazael to be the next king of Syria, Jehu to be the next king of Israel, and Elisha to be My prophet after you."

Elijah hung his head as God spoke. Now he was ashamed that he was hiding from Jezebel. God had important work for him to do.

"By the way, you are not the last faithful follower," God added. "There are still seven thousand men in Israel who follow Me."

Elijah left Mount Horeb as quickly as he could. Who had time to hide in a cave now? He had important things to do for God, and he had better get started!

WHAT DO YOU THINK?
What this story teaches: God does not have to shout; some of His most important messages are whispered.

1. Why did Elijah run away to Mount Horeb and hide in a cave? Who was he running from? Why was he afraid?
2. What did God tell Elijah there? Did He shout or whisper that message? What did He tell Elijah to do? Did he do it?

A Five-Star Production

"I think we should put on a five-star production," BoBo suggested. "It will really wow them all!"

"This is not a TV special," Pookie argued. "It's our class presentation for Promotion Sunday. You don't need such a big deal for a Sunday school program."

"It's more important than a TV program," Bobo argued back. "So we should make it more spectacular."

"Like what?" Maxi asked.

"We'll borrow a tape deck and play a grand march while we march in," BoBo began. "Then we'll get some stage lights from school to highlight each kid who does something. We'll have a full orchestra on tape as background music while we present a play about life at Sunday school this year. When our teacher introduces each kid we will have a live drummer give a long drum roll. Then..."

"BoBo! Stop!" said Maxi. "That's awful. Ask our teacher. She will tell you."

"Yeah, what about BoBo's suggestion?" Pookie asked.

The teacher smiled. "Our lesson today is about BoBo's suggestion," she said. "It was in the Bible long before BoBo thought of it."

"It WAS?" BoBo asked, his eyes wide open. "Wow! Where?"

"Well, there was a prophet named Elijah who went into a mountain," the teacher began. "He wanted God to say something to him. Since it was God who would speak, Elijah thought the whole thing should be a five-star production."

"Like stage lights and drums rolling?" asked Maxi.

"Something like that," the teacher said with a smile. "He thought that God should say what He wanted to say with a five-star production wind that tore up the mountains. But do you think that God spoke through that wind?"

"Did He?" asked Pookie.

"The Bible says He didn't," the teacher answered. "Then Elijah thought God would say what He wanted to say through a five-star earthquake that shook up the mountain."

"Did He?" asked BoBo.

"The Bible says He didn't," the teacher answered. "Then Elijah listened for a bigger and better five-star production so God could speak through that. Suddenly he heard God speaking. Do you know how God spoke?"

"A tornado!" said Pookie.

"An atom bomb!" said BoBo.

"A fleet of jet airplanes," suggested Maxi.

"All wrong," said the teacher. "Elijah listened and listened and listened. Then suddenly he heard a quiet whisper. It was God saying what He wanted to say."

"Wow! Maybe we should forget our five-star production for Promotion Sunday," BoBo said quietly.

"But who's going to whisper for us?" asked Pookie.

"Maxi!" suggested BoBo. "Except he doesn't really need to whisper. Why can't he just quietly tell some important things God has done for us this year?"

"Good idea!" said the teacher. "That will be even better than a five-star production."

"Maybe it's a six-star one!" said BoBo.

LET'S TALK ABOUT THIS
What this story teaches: Some of God's most important messages, and ours, are whispered, not shouted.

1. Do you ever feel that everything has to be a five-star production, like a TV special, in order to keep you interested? What about some of the quiet things of life? Can they be interesting too?

2. Sometimes our quiet moments with God are times when He can say the most to us. Think about that the next time you have to have a TV special to keep you interested.

Someone to Do My Work

1 Kings 19:19-21

"I have worked hard for You," Elijah told the Lord. "But the people won't listen to me. They have torn down Your altars and killed Your prophets. Now I'm the only one of Your followers left, and they are trying to kill me, too."

Elijah felt sorry for himself when he told the Lord those things. He thought that nobody cared about all his work. He thought that it wasn't really important.

Actually Elijah was one of the greatest of God's workers since the days of Moses. He had brought down fire from heaven, caused oil and meal jars to stay full, and even raised a boy from the dead.

Now God was sending him home to anoint two kings and to anoint a prophet to take his place. That was certainly important work!

Naturally Elijah was concerned about the kind of men he would anoint to be the next king of Syria and the next king of Israel. Kings led the countries they ruled. Their way of ruling was important to all the people of the lands.

But Elijah must have wondered more about that fellow Elisha, whom God said he should anoint to do his work when he was gone.

What kind of a person was he?

What kind of work would he do?

What kind of prophet would he be?

How loyal would he be to the Lord?

How well would he serve the people?

Elijah wondered about those and many other things as he went to find Elisha. Somehow he knew where Elisha was and found him plowing a field with twelve teams of oxen.

Elijah watched Elisha for a while, then walked through the field. He took his mantle, something like a big cape, and threw it over Elisha's shoulders.

Elisha knew from this that he would become Elijah's helper and then would do Elijah's work when he was gone. It was a way of saying, "You will do my work after me."

"Let me first say good-bye to my family," Elisha told Elijah.

"Go ahead," Elijah told him.

Then Elisha killed two oxen and made a fire with his wooden plow. He roasted the meat of the oxen and served it to the men who had been plowing with him.

With his oxen and his plow gone, Elisha's days as a farmer were over. He could not turn back now. He could not go back to the farm again. He would be God's prophet for as long as he lived.

Elijah knew now that Elisha would follow the Lord completely, as he had done. But he could not know then the mighty things that Elisha would do for the Lord.

WHAT DO YOU THINK?
What this story teaches: When God's workers must choose others to take their place, they have an important job to do.

1. What kind of a person was Elijah? Did he follow God as he should? Did he do good work for Him?
2. What kind of person do you think Elijah wanted to do his work when he was gone? If you had been Elijah, what would you have thought when you threw your mantle over Elisha's shoulders?

The New King

There was once a wise king who ruled a good land far away. But as he grew older he decided to choose a new king to rule when he was gone.

"I must choose the right person to rule in my place," said the king. "I must be sure that he will rule wisely and well."

So the king called for the three bravest knights of the land. "I will choose one of you to rule this good land when I am gone," the king told them. "But first I will send you on a mission. You will each visit the shepherd who lives at the edge of the forest and will rule him for one day. Whoever rules him best will be the next king."

The following morning Sir Mighty put on his armor and rode forth from the king's castle. In the late morning he arrived at the edge of the forest and saw the shepherd with his sheep.

"Welcome, brave knight," the shepherd called. "What may I do for you?"

"It is not for you to ask," Sir Mighty said harshly. "I will give the orders, and you will obey me, or I will kill your flocks and burn your hut. A good king must demand absolute obedience."

The second morning Sir Greedy put a big sack on his horse and rode forth from the king's castle. In the late morning he arrived at the edge of the forest and saw the shepherd with his sheep.

"Welcome, brave knight," the shepherd called. "What may I do for you?"

"It is not for you to ask," said Sir Greedy. "I will tell you what I want. You will give me half of your flocks and the fruit in your orchards and vineyards. You may rule yourself as long as I get those things."

The third morning Sir Kindly rode forth from the king's castle. In the late morning he arrived at the edge of the forest and saw the shepherd with his sheep.

"Welcome, brave knight," the shepherd called. "What may I do for you?"

"Will you be my shepherd today?" Sir Kindly asked. "I want to serve my king's people well, and who can teach me how to lead them better than a shepherd?"

All that day Sir Kindly listened eagerly to the good shepherd tell how to lead and serve the people well. At the end of the day he said good-bye.

"Thank you, good shepherd," said Sir Kindly. "May I come again to hear your wisdom?"

"You may come again, and you will lead your people well," the shepherd said.

The fourth morning the three knights went to the throne room to wait for the king. They were anxious to hear which he would choose to rule when he was gone.

"I'm sure he will choose me," Sir Mighty said. "A good king demands obedience."

"No, he will choose me," Sir Greedy said. "A good king must be a wealthy king and must keep his subjects poor. Then he does not need to bother ruling over them."

Sir Kindly said nothing. He was still thinking of all the wonderful things the good shepherd had told

him. He hoped the king would choose him, for he was eager to serve and lead the people like a shepherd would lead his sheep, but he knew that was for the king to decide.

Suddenly the door opened. But instead of the king, it was the shepherd who walked in. The three knights gasped with surprise as the shepherd took off his rough cloak and sat down upon the king's throne.

"The king!" they all shouted together.

"Yes, the shepherd and the king are the same person," said the king. "A good king must lead and serve his people like a good shepherd, not like a cruel or greedy master. Sir Mighty and Sir Greedy, bow before Sir Kindly, the new king."

LET'S TALK ABOUT THIS
What this story teaches: Good leaders serve their people well.

1. Why was it important for the good king to find the right person to rule when he was gone? How did he find that person? Why do you think he chose Sir Kindly?
2. Why was it so important for Elijah to find the right prophet to serve God when he was gone? How did he show Elisha that he was that prophet?

STORIES THAT JESUS TOLD

Samaritan on the Road

Luke 10:25-37

One day a man tried to trick Jesus with some questions. He was an expert on religious law. He wanted Jesus to say the wrong thing about the law so that people would not follow Him.

"What must I do to live forever?" the man asked.

"You should know the answer to that," Jesus replied. "What do you find in the law?"

"Love the Lord your God with all your heart, soul, strength, and mind. Love your neighbor as much as you love yourself," the man replied.

"You have given the right answer to your own question," Jesus told him. "If you do this, you will live forever."

But the man still wanted to trick Jesus. So he asked another question.

"Who is my neighbor?" he asked.

Jesus then told this story to answer the man's question:

"One of our own Jewish men was traveling on the road from Jerusalem to Jericho when he was attacked by robbers. They took his clothes and money, beat him up, and left him half dead by the road.

"Not long after that, one of our own priests came along the road. When he saw this injured man lying there, he passed by on the other side of the road. Then a Levite, who helps in our Jewish religious work, came by. He took one look at the poor man, then went on his way.

"After that, a Samaritan came down the road. As you know, you people all hate the Samaritans. But when he saw this poor man lying beside the road, he felt sorry for him. He knelt down, put some medicine on his wounds, and bandaged them. Then he laid the man carefully on his donkey and took him to an inn.

"The Samaritan stayed with this poor injured man until he was sure that he was all right. The next day

he gave the innkeeper two coins, worth two days' wages, and told him to take care of the man while he was gone.

"'If you must spend more to get this fellow well, I will pay you when I return,' the Samaritan told the innkeeper."

When Jesus had finished His story, He looked at the expert in Jewish law, who had tried to trick Him. "Which of these three men was a good neighbor to the injured man?"

"The one who was kind to him and helped him," the man answered.

"Then you must go and be that kind of neighbor, too," Jesus told him.

WHAT DO YOU THINK?
What this story teaches: A good friend or neighbor takes time to help those with special needs.

1. Why would you expect the priest to help the poor injured man? Why would you expect the Levite to help him? Why would you not expect the Samaritan to help?
2. Which one did help the injured man? Why do you think he stopped to help? What did he do?
3. What did this show about the Samaritan? Why is he sometimes called the "Good Samaritan?"

Maxi, the Good Samaritan

"Why do I have to go to the grocery store for Mommi?" Maxi grumbled. Maxi was still in a grumbly mood when he came to the stoplight by the grocery store.

"Look at that lady by the stoplight," Maxi mumbled under his breath. "She must be eighty years old, at least, and she's gone to the grocery store by herself. So why did Mommi need me?"

Maxi watched the lady for a while. The light turned green, and the lady started across the street. But when she heard a horn honk she quickly stepped back on the sidewalk. The light turned red, and the lady waited. But when it turned green the lady took one step into the street and then went back on the sidewalk again.

"Looks like she needs help crossing the street," Maxi said to himself. "The problem is that I don't have time now. I have to get Mommi's groceries."

Maxi hurried into the grocery store. Within five minutes he had the few things chosen, paid for, and in a bag to carry home.

When he came out of the grocery store, Maxi was surprised to see the lady still standing by the curb, waiting to cross the street. "Why doesn't someone help her across?" Maxi complained. "What's the matter with people? I sure would, but I have to get home with these groceries."

Maxi hurried down the street with his bag of groceries. But when he came to the end of the block and looked back, he saw the lady still standing there.

"I can't believe it!" Maxi mumbled. "Still no one has helped her. Everyone has an excuse!"

Then suddenly Maxi realized what he had said. Maxi stopped and watched the lady.

Why couldn't HE help her? Was he really in such a hurry to get the groceries and get home? Or was that just an excuse?

Maxi turned and went back to the place where the lady stood. "May I help you cross the street?" he asked.

"What a sweet boy," the lady said with a smile. "I have cataracts and can't see as well as I should, so

I'm often afraid to cross a street until someone helps me."

Maxi took the lady's arm and, as soon as the light turned green, led her across the street.

"Thank you! Thank you!" the lady said. "You are such a good boy. Some other boy went past me before and went into the grocery store and wouldn't even offer to help me. Another boy came out of the store, and he wouldn't offer to help me either. I'm so glad you're not like those thoughtless boys!"

Maxi gulped when the lady said that. He was sorry he had thought he was in such a hurry that he couldn't help her. Then Maxi realized that the lady had been holding a bag of groceries all this time.

"Aren't those groceries getting too heavy for you?" Maxi asked.

"They certainly are!" the lady said. "But what can I do about it?"

"Give them to me," said Maxi. "I'll carry them home for you."

"Thank you for your help. You're a Good Samaritan!" the lady said when they reached her house. "Not at all like those other two boys."

"A good what?" asked Maxi.

"Good Samaritan," said the lady. "You know, the story in the Bible about the Samaritan who stopped to help."

Then Maxi remembered the Bible story they had read together as a family. He remembered the two men who had passed the injured man and felt ashamed that he had been like them. He remembered how Jesus said the Good Samaritan was a good neighbor.

From now on I'll try to be a Good Samaritan at all times, Maxi thought. Then he waved good-bye and hurried home with Mommi's groceries.

LET'S TALK ABOUT THIS

What this story teaches: We should take time to help those with special needs, for that will please Jesus.

1. Why do you think Maxi passed by the lady at first? Why did he go back to help her?
2. If you had been Maxi, how would you have felt when the lady said, "I'm so glad you're not like those thoughtless boys?" How would you have felt when she said, "You're a Good Samaritan!"
3. Look for ways this week to be a Good Samaritan. You'll be surprised when you see how many there are!

First Things First

Luke 10:38-42

"Martha! Martha! Look who is coming!" Mary called.

Martha was excited, too, as she looked down the road. Jesus was coming! Mary and Martha were always happy to see Him come for a visit.

Mary and Martha were sisters. They and their brother, Lazarus, lived in the little village of Bethany, just east of Jerusalem, over the Mount of Olives. Often, when Jesus came to Jerusalem, He stopped to see them. They were His good friends.

But before Jesus reached the door, Martha began to worry about lunch. "What will we feed Jesus?" she wondered. "And look at the house! I must straighten things up before He gets here."

Martha was so busy cleaning and fixing and doing fussy things that she hardly had time to say hello. But as soon as she did, she quickly ran to the kitchen.

Mary didn't care at all about lunch. She didn't even care if she ate lunch. To her the most important thing in the world right now was to talk with Jesus. She wanted to ask Him so many questions and listen while He told about His home in heaven and His Father who lived there.

Martha rushed to and fro in the kitchen. She filled this pot with water and stirred things in another one. She clattered and banged things around without hearing a word that Jesus said.

Suddenly Martha realized that she was doing all the work while Mary was doing nothing. The more

she fussed around with things, the more this bothered her. At last she came into the room where Mary sat by Jesus' feet, listening carefully.

"Lord, doesn't it bother You that my sister is letting me do all the work?" she asked. It was a bit rude to ask this important guest such a question, but she did it anyway.

One might think at this point that Jesus would smile and tell Mary to go help her sister get lunch. But Jesus really didn't care if He ate lunch either. He thought it was much more important to tell Mary the things she wanted to know.

"Martha, Martha," Jesus answered. "You're so busy and bothered doing all those things. Don't you see that Mary has chosen what is most important? I will not take that away from her."

Nobody knows if Martha went back to the kitchen or sat down with Mary to listen to Jesus. But she certainly learned that it is much more important to listen to Jesus than to eat lunch. That is putting first things first.

WHAT DO YOU THINK?
What this story teaches: Jesus should be put first above all things.

1. What did Martha do when Jesus came to visit? What did Mary do?
2. Which did Jesus say was more important? How did Mary put first things first? What did you learn from this story?

Out of the Treasure Chest

"Grandmommi! What an exciting attic you have!" Mini almost shouted.

"Yeah, it's just full of old things," Maxi added. "Where did you get all these?"

Grandmommi laughed. "When you live in one house all these years, you collect a lot of things," she said. "And most of them find their way to the attic."

Maxi and Mini looked at an old butter churn that Grandmommi had used when she was a little girl. They saw a typewriter that Grandpoppi had used many years ago, before he bought a new one. And they talked with Grandmommi about a dress form that she had used when she had sewn her own clothes.

"What's in that old chest?" Maxi asked.

"That's our treasure chest," Grandmommi said with a twinkle in her eye.

"TREASURE chest?" Maxi asked, his mouth falling open. "You mean it's full of old gold coins and stuff from a pirate ship?"

"Not quite," said Grandmommi. "Who wants old stuffy gold coins and pirate treasure?"

"I do!" said Maxi.

"Me, too," said Mini.

"Anyone can get gold coins and pirate treasure," said Grandmommi. "The treasure in that chest is worth far more to us than those things."

Maxi's mouth fell open again, and Mini's eyes were as big as saucers.

"Wow!"

"Treasure more valuable than pirate treasure!"

"It must be worth a fortune!"

"Maybe it's diamonds and rubies and things!"

"What IS it, Grandmommi?"

71

Grandmommi laughed. "Treasure isn't always money," she said softly. "Some of the richest treasures of life can't be spent at the store. Our treasure chest doesn't hold money or jewels or gold but something worth more to us than all these things."

"May we see your treasure, Grandmommi?" Maxi asked.

"Open the lid, Maxi and Mini, and I will show you our treasure," said Grandmommi.

Maxi and Mini opened the lid slowly. Then their mouths fell open even wider with surprise.

"There's nothing but old books and clothes," said Mini.

"I don't see ANY treasure," Maxi added. "Where is it?"

Grandmommi lifted an old dress from the chest. "This is my wedding dress," she said. "I wore it when I promised your Grandpoppi I would be his bride."

"May I put it on?" Mini asked.

"Of course," said Grandmommi.

Mini wiggled into the old dress and looked at herself in a big mirror leaning against an old dresser. She giggled as she saw herself in the old-fashioned wedding dress.

"You make a lovely bride!" Grandmommi said.

"Yuk!" said Maxi.

Grandmommi took an old photo album from the chest. "Family treasures," she said softly. "Pictures of my grandmother and grandfather and their families."

One after another, family treasures were taken from the old chest. There were beautiful doilies, which Grandmommi's mother had made. There was also a gold watch, which Grandpoppi's father had received as a Christmas gift many years before.

"Here is one of my greatest treasures of all," said Grandmommi as she took out a small white Bible. When I was a little girl, I read from this Bible every day. I memorized verses from this. And with this Bible my poppi helped me accept Jesus as my Savior and taught me to put Jesus first in all I do."

Maxi and Mini were quiet for several moments as they looked through the Bible. They smiled as they saw a picture of Grandmommi as a little girl, holding the Bible.

"You're right, Grandmommi," Maxi said with a smile as he gave the Bible back to her.

"About what?" asked Grandmommi.

"These treasures are worth far more than a chest full of pirate gold," said Maxi.

"I think so, too," said Mini. "And I'm going to save the Bible I'm reading to show my grandchildren! I want them to know that I put Jesus first in all I do, too."

Maxi and Grandmommi smiled as they thought of Mini's grandchildren, who would some day take today's Muffin Family treasures out of a treasure chest.

LET'S TALK ABOUT THIS
What this story teaches: Life's greatest treasures are those that help us put Jesus first.

1. Why are family treasures like those Grandmommi showed worth more than money? Do you have family treasures like those in your family?
2. Why was Grandmommi's Bible so special? Why was Mini's Bible special too? How do you think each Bible helped Grandmommi or Mini put Jesus first in all she did?
3. Are you reading your Bible each day? Has someone helped you accept Jesus as your Savior and encouraged you to put Him first in all you do?

NEW LIFE!

Waiting for God to Work

Acts 1-2

For a long time the disciples stood quietly on the Mount of Olives, watching the sky where Jesus had gone up into heaven. He had talked about such things while He was with them, but they somehow did not expect Him to leave that way.

They may have stayed there for hours. Nobody knows. But they knew that He would not come back. He was gone. They had seen Him go.

"Now what do we do?" someone must have asked, breaking the silence.

"Go back to Jerusalem and wait, as He told us to do," someone answered.

"For what?"

"For that special power He said would come."

"When? How?"

"Who knows?"

Nobody knew. But together they walked down the Mount of Olives, crossed the Kidron Valley, and went up into the city. They returned to the upper room where they had eaten the Last Supper together.

One person began to pray, then another followed, and another. Before long, a prayer meeting had begun. They prayed about many things, with both men and women taking part.

While they were there, Peter reminded the others of how Judas had betrayed Jesus and then killed himself. He reminded them that Judas had returned the money to the priests at the Temple and that they had bought a burial ground with the money.

"Now we need to choose a man to take Judas's place," Peter told them. With a system called "casting lots," they chose a man named Matthias. He then became an apostle, along with the other eleven.

There must have been more praying and more business to take care of. Certainly there was much talk about all the things that had happened in their lives since Jesus was crucified. This went on until the day of Pentecost arrived.

Pentecost was a great festival, held once each year in Israel. The harvest was over, and there was much rejoicing. From all over Israel, men gathered with their families in Jerusalem to celebrate.

It had been exactly fifty days since Jesus had eaten the Last Supper in this upper room with His followers. Now they waited to see what would happen.

Suddenly there was a sound like a mighty wind, which filled the room where they were meeting.

"Look on our heads!" someone shouted.

When the people looked around the room, they saw a little flame of fire on each person's head. Then, as suddenly as the sound of wind and the flames of fire had appeared, the people began to speak in different languages.

News of those miracles spread quickly to the people in the streets. Those people had gathered in Jerusalem from many lands. Naturally, they were amazed to hear the disciples speak their languages as clearly as they did.

"These people are all from Galilee," they said. "But they are speaking our languages perfectly! How do they do it?"

The answer should have been clear. They were filled with the Holy Spirit. Only He could do that.

Peter explained that to the people in a sermon. Their Scriptures had said that the Holy Spirit would come. Now He was here! They must decide to accept Him or not. "Repent, turn from your sin, and be baptized every one of you in the name of Jesus Christ," Peter told them. "He will take away your sin, and you shall receive the Holy Spirit."

After Peter's long sermon, 3,000 people accepted Jesus into their lives and received the Holy Spirit. Then they joined the other believers in praying together and working together for the Lord.

Many wonderful things were done in those days, for the Lord was among those people. It was a time of great joy.

WHAT DO YOU THINK?
What this story teaches: The Holy Spirit has come to enter our lives, walk with us, and help us live as we should for the Lord.

1. After Jesus went back to heaven, how did His followers spend their time in the upper room? What were they waiting for?
2. How did those people know when the Holy Spirit came? What happened?

The King's Friend

Once in a land far away a king made a proclamation that was sent far and wide. "Whoever passes the test I give shall rule with me and be my friend," the king's proclamation read.

Three princes came from nearby lands to meet the king, each hoping to pass the test.

First, Prince One bowed before the king.

"My test is simple, Prince One," said the king. "There is a road that leads from here to that mountain over there. You must carry this heavy bag there before the sun sets in the western sky. You may try it yourself, or you may wait for my friend to come to help you."

Prince One picked up the heavy bag and waved good-bye. "I will go alone," he said. "I do not need your friend to help me."

Then Prince Two bowed before the king.

"My test is simple, Prince Two," said the king. "There is a road that leads from here to that mountain over there. You must carry this heavy bag there before the sun sets in the western sky. You may try it yourself, or you may wait for my friend to come to help you."

"I will wait awhile for your friend to come," said Prince Two. Then he took his heavy bag and sat by the side of the road.

After that, Prince Three bowed before the king.

"My test is simple, Prince Three," said the king. "There is a road that leads from here to that mountain over there. You must carry this heavy bag there before the sun sets in the western sky. You may try it yourself, or you may wait for my friend to come to help you."

"I, too, will wait for your friend to come," said Prince Three. Then he took his heavy bag and sat by the side of the road.

The morning sun rose higher and higher in the sky. With each passing moment Prince Two grew more impatient. "Where is the king's friend?" he asked often, complaining more as time passed.

Toward midmorning, Prince Two stood up and threw his heavy bag upon his shoulder. "I will wait no longer," he said. "Prince One has already gone far. If I do not leave now, I will not get there by sunset." So, saying that, Prince Two walked quickly away, leaving Prince Three waiting beside the road.

"The king told me to wait for his friend," said Prince Three. "I'm sure he will keep his promise and send his friend to help."

Late that morning, as high noon was near, Prince Three felt a gust of wind in the trees. He looked up quickly and saw a mighty man approach.

"The king has sent me to help you," the mighty man said. "Shoulder your heavy bag and when it grows too heavy, I will carry it for you. If you grow too weary and can't go on, I will lift you up and carry you."

As the day passed, Prince Three carried his bag whenever he could, for it was his to carry. But whenever it grew too heavy for him, the king's friend lifted it from him until he was able to bear it again. And when Prince Three grew too weak at times to go on, the king's mighty friend lifted him and carried him until he was strong again.

"How could I walk this road without you, mighty friend?" said Prince Three. "You have carried my burdens, you have lifted me up when I have been weary, and you have been a friend and counselor along the way. You have filled me with joy and gladness and led me into pleasant bypaths I would not have known."

The king's friend smiled and pointed to the mountain ahead. They would soon be there, long before sunset.

"What about Prince One and Prince Two?" asked Prince Three. "Have they reached the mountain?"

The king's friend shook his head. "No one can walk this way and bear the burden given him without my help."

Then the wise prince was even more glad that he had patiently waited for the king's mighty friend. Now he would rule with the king and be his friend.

LET'S TALK ABOUT THIS
What this story teaches: We cannot walk life's way as Christians without the Holy Spirit to go with us and help us.

1. How does this story remind you of the disciples' waiting for the coming of the Holy Spirit?
2. How does the king's mighty friend remind you of the Holy Spirit?
3. Is it possible to walk life's way as a Christian without the Holy Spirit to help us? Why not?

Living Together God's Way

Acts 2: 41-47

"Why are they so different from our other neighbors?" some of the people in Jerusalem asked.

They were talking about Jesus' followers. They were different because they had turned from their sins and asked Jesus to be their Savior and Lord. They had invited the Holy Spirit into their lives.

Jesus had told His followers what would happen. "You will receive power when the Holy Spirit comes," Jesus had said, "and you will be witnesses for Me."

That is what their friends and neighbors saw. That is why they were different from other friends and neighbors.

Most neighbors tried to earn as much and keep as much as possible. The believers were giving it away. Most neighbors tried to do things to help themselves. The believers were doing all they could to help others. Most neighbors were bragging about themselves and their families. The believers were telling others how wonderful Jesus was and how the Holy Spirit had changed their lives.

There was something else different. Most neighbors were never very happy. They complained about this and grumbled about that. There was never enough of some things and always too much of other things. But the believers were the happiest people in town.

No wonder the friends and neighbors said they were different! No wonder those friends and neighbors began to wonder if they should become believers also.

Day by day more people accepted Jesus and invited the Holy Spirit to go with them. Day by day more people joined in friendship and fellowship with Jesus' followers, praying with them, working with them, and helping them help Jesus.

No wonder there was such excitement among the believers!

WHAT DO YOU THINK?
What this story teaches: To live at peace with your friends and neighbors means you must first be at peace with Jesus.

1. In what ways were the believers different from their other friends and neighbors? What caused them to be different?
2. What effect did this have on their friends and neighbors? Will it affect your friends and neighbors the same way?

Mini Happy Returns

"Happy birthday, Mrs. Grump!" Mini Muffin said to the pretend Mrs. Grump in her mirror, who was really just Mini's reflection.

"Why, thank you, dearie." Mrs. Grump smiled sweetly at Mrs. Crump, who was the really-truly Mini Muffin pretending to be Mrs. Crump.

"Since you're such a sweet friend, I thought I would make you a devil's food cake for your birthday, my dear Mrs. Grump," said Mrs. Crump.

"DEVIL'S food? Of all the nerve! Is that what you think of me, dearie? And why not ANGEL food?"

"Hrummfp! Angel! Show me your wings, and I'll make you angel food cake. And were you an angel last week when you gossiped to the neighbors about me?"

"Oh, so now I'm a gossip! I'm mortified! I was just telling my neighbors some important things about my DEAR friend."

87

With each part of the conversation Mini raised her voice one note on the scale and one notch in volume. By this time she had waked up Ruff and Tuff, who had been sleeping in opposite corners of the room. Ruff snarled and jumped up beside Mrs. Crump. Tuff arched her back, hissed, and jumped up beside Mrs. Grump in Mini's mirror.

Each time Mrs. Grump shouted at Mrs. Crump, Tuff arched her back and hissed. Each time Mrs. Crump shouted at Mrs. Grump, Ruff raised his hair, snarled, and barked back at Tuff.

Before long, Mrs. Grump and Mrs. Crump had become nasty with each other. Mrs. Grump was saying some very un-Muffinlike things to Mrs. Crump, and Mrs. Crump was saying some very un-Muffinlike things to Mrs. Grump.

As things became loud and hot, Tuff grew more and more angry, too. Ruff became almost as nasty as Mrs. Crump. Suddenly Tuff became so angry that she jumped on Ruff and began to scratch his nose. Then Ruff got her on the floor and began to teach her how an angry dog fights.

"Happy grouchday!" Mrs. Crump screamed at Mrs. Grump.

"You're as half-baked as your cakes, dearie!" Mrs. Grump screamed back at Mrs. Crump.

At the loudest and worst part of the Grump-Crump-Ruff-Tuff argument, Mommi walked in. Her mouth fell open when she saw and heard all that was going on.

"WHAT is happening in here?" Mommi almost had to shout above the noise.

Suddenly Mrs. Grump smiled sweetly at Mrs. Crump and thanked her for the LOVEly devil's food cake, which caused Mrs. Crump to smile just as sweetly and assure Mrs. Grump that her angel food cake would be simply DElicious.

Just as suddenly Ruff stopped fighting Tuff, and Tuff stopped fighting Ruff. Ruff plopped down in his corner, looked once more at Tuff with one cautious eye, yawned, and went to sleep. Tuff plopped down in her basket, looked once more at Ruff with one cautious eye, yawned, and went to sleep.

"NOW, Mini Muffin, please tell me what was going on in here?"

"Oh, nothing much, Mommi. We were just having a little birthday party. But it did get out of hand, so we'll tell everyone to be sweet to each other from now on."

"Hm. All right, then. Mini happy returns!"

LET'S TALK ABOUT THIS

What this story teaches: Living in unity and harmony with friends, family, and neighbors starts with us.

1. What happened when Mrs. Grump shouted at Mrs. Crump? What happened when Mrs. Grump or Mrs. Crump was sweet with the other? What happened when Ruff or Tuff snarled or growled at each other? What happened when they were sweet with each other?

2. How do others usually respond when you are nasty or angry with them? How do they usually respond when you are happy and pleasant with them? What does this tell you about the best way to live in unity and harmony with friends, family, or neighbors?

3. Which way do you think pleases God most—when you are nasty with others or pleasant with them? Why?

A Much Better Gift

Acts 3

"Alms for the poor! Alms for the poor!"

The poor man sat by the gate that led into the Temple in Jerusalem. He was crippled, and at that time crippled people could not find a job. It was hard for even a strong, healthy man to find enough work to feed his family. So a crippled man, like a blind or deaf man, almost always had to become a beggar.

That was the way he did it. All day he sat by a gate or beside a road and asked people for "alms," gifts of money for himself and his family.

"Alms for the poor!" he cried out when Peter and John entered the Temple. It was three o'clock in the afternoon, a time when people went to the Temple for prayer.

Most of the people passed by the beggar without giving him a thing. After all, this fellow had been sitting here by the gate each day for many years. Some days they gave him a coin, and some days they didn't.

Peter and John stopped. Peter stared at him, while the man kept on crying out for alms.

Suddenly the man realized that Peter was staring at him. He stopped his noisy cries. But he would not look into Peter's eyes.

"Look at me!" Peter commanded.

Slowly the beggar looked up at Peter. His eyes looked into Peter's eyes. Then he slowly held out his hand for the coin he thought Peter would give him.

"I have no silver or gold coins to give you," Peter said quietly. The man's eyes dropped again. He was ready to start crying out for alms.

"But I have a much better gift," Peter went on. "In the name of Jesus Christ of Nazareth, get up and walk!"

As he said this, Peter reached out his hand and lifted the man up to his feet. The man trembled as he stood, but suddenly he felt strength coming into his legs. He took one step forward, then two, then walked about, shouting with joy. Before long he was leaping about as though he had never been crippled.

"Praise God!" he shouted. "Praise God for healing me!"

Imagine how surprised the people in the Temple were when this man ran through the courtyards, shouting and leaping as he went.

"Praise God!" he kept on shouting.

He had expected a coin from Peter and John. But the gift he received was a much better gift! That's the way God does things when we are willing to receive His better gifts.

WHAT DO YOU THINK?

What this story teaches: God has much better gifts for us than we expect.

1. What happened when the crippled man asked Peter and John for a coin? What did Peter give him instead? Was it a much better gift?

2. What do you think this man thought the next morning? Would he rather have had a coin than his much better gift?

3. God has wonderful gifts to give us. Be careful that you do not want "things" more, for they are worth far less than His much better gifts. Can you name some of the much better gifts He has for you?

The Old Key

"Help me, kind sir! Any small coin will do!"

The poor man sat beside the road, begging for coins so that he might buy food. He was hungry and tired, almost too tired to look up into the kind face of the prince who had stopped beside him.

"I do not have one coin with me," said the prince. "All I have is this old key. It is yours. Take it, use it wisely, and you will have something worth far more than coins."

The poor man looked up at the face of the prince. It was so warm and kind that he stared at it for a long time. The prince smiled and held out the old key. Then the poor man reached up with a trembling hand and took it from him.

"Thank you, kind sir," said the poor man. "How shall I use it?"

"You will find the way if you are truly wise," said the prince. Then he went on, leaving the poor man with the key.

The poor man watched the prince until he was out of sight. Then he began to look closely at the old

93

key. He noticed a strange fruit carved on the key. Beside the fruit were the words "By Me if any man enter in, he shall be saved."

"I have read those words before," said the poor man. "But where?"

As the poor man thought about the key he remembered the words of the prince, "Use it wisely, and you will have something worth far more than coins."

"How can I use it?" he wondered. "And where?" Then the poor man realized that he could not use the key sitting beside the road.

"I must follow that kind man," he said. "The key must surely be used where he is."

The poor man struggled to his feet and went down the road where the prince had gone. Along the way he saw a high stone wall with a great wooden door in it. At the top of the door, carved into the wood, was the same fruit that was on the key. Beside it were the words "I am the Door."

The poor man looked at the old key and then at the door. The fruit was certainly the same. As he read the words on the door first and then the words on the key, he noticed how they fit together.

"I am the Door. By Me if any man enter in, he shall be saved."

Then the poor man saw a keyhole, shaped exactly like his old key. *Dare I try it?* he wondered.

With his hand trembling, the poor man slipped the old key into the keyhole. It fit exactly. Slowly he turned the key and pushed open the great door.

The poor man stared with surprise as he saw a beautiful land filled with rich vineyards and orchards. And there before him was a sparkling stream. Beside it was a great banquet table, filled with the most wonderful food he had ever seen, a banquet fit for a king.

"I have been waiting for you," a voice said. "I have prepared this table for you in this green pasture, beside these still waters. Come, wash in the cool water, anoint your head with this sweet-smelling oil, and dine with me."

The poor man's hands were still trembling as he sat down to dine with the prince. "Must I leave when I have eaten?" he asked sadly. "Or may I stay?"

The prince pointed to the great wooden door. On the inside of the door were carved these words: "And shall go in and out, and find pasture."

"You are free to come and go as you wish," said the prince.

"Surely goodness and mercy have followed me into this land where you dwell," said the poor man. Then he bowed before the prince to worship him.

LET'S TALK ABOUT THIS
What this story teaches: We may have riches beyond our dreams if we will only receive what God offers us.

1. How does this story remind you of Peter and John's healing the lame man at the Temple? Read Psalm 23. How does this story remind you of this psalm?
2. Who is "the Door?" Read John 10:9. What are some of life's greatest riches that God offers us? Have you received them?

Mini's Word List

Twelve words that all Minis and Maxis want to know.

ALMS—In Bible times there were many poor people. Those who were blind or crippled almost never got a job. Governments did not take care of these people, as many do today. So these people had to beg, asking others who could work to give them coins or food or other gifts. These gifts, or kind deeds, were called alms (pronounced AHMS).

ALTAR—Before Jesus came, people in Israel burned animals on an altar as a way of asking God to take away their sin. Some altars were made of stones. Others were made of wood, covered with a metal such as bronze. Others were made of metal only. Incense was also burned on small altars.

BURNT OFFERING—A young bull or lamb was often killed and its meat burned on an altar. That was a way of asking God to take away sin. There were many different ways of doing this. But usually the animal took the place of the person who offered it, symbolically paying the price for his or her sins.

FELLOWSHIP—A "fellow" may be a special friend. Those who follow Jesus become special friends with each other because He becomes a special Friend to each of them. This special friendship among Jesus' followers is called "fellowship," for they enjoy being with each other and doing things together, especially things that honor Jesus.

HEIR—Someone who receives a person's money and other possessions when he or she dies. Usually the heir is a child. In Bible times it was especially the oldest son, who received more than his brothers and sisters.

HOPE—We have hope when we expect good things to happen instead of bad things. Jesus brings hope to His followers, for even though things may look bad, we know that all things will work out for the best with Him. Our best hope is to live with Him in His home in heaven, free from our sins.

OBEY, OBEDIENCE—Most people put their own wants first. Some put what God wants first, or what parents want. To put God's wants, or parents' wants, before ours is a good way to obey. In this way, obedience is more than just doing what someone tells us to do, although it is that, too.

PENTECOST—Each year the people of Israel had three special feasts, or festivals. All men were expected to go to them. The first, Passover, was in April. It celebrated the time when the Israelites left Egypt under Moses. The second, Pentecost, was fifty days later. It celebrated the end of the spring wheat harvest. The third, Tabernacles, in October, celebrated the end of the autumn harvest.

PROPHET—In Old Testament times special men were called by God to tell their people what He said. Sometimes they told their people what would happen later—often hundreds of years later.

TRIBE—All the people who descended from one person belonged to a "tribe" named for that person. In the Bible this usually meant one of the twelve sons of Jacob. For example, the tribe of Judah included all people descended from Jacob's son Judah.

UNITY—Living together and working together for one purpose. Christians should have unity, for we all belong to Jesus and should try to live as He wants us to.

WITNESSES—People who tell what they have seen or what has happened to them are witnesses. Jesus' followers should be witnesses, telling what they know about Jesus and what He has done for them.